S0-DZB-911

CCSS Genre Realistic Fiction

Essential Question
What makes you laugh?

Funny Faces

by Elizabeth Brereton
illustrated by Caroline Romanet

D1520162

Chapter 1
Missing Out

Max walked through the front door and went into the kitchen. "Hi, Mom, I'm home!"

"How was school?" Mom asked.

"Great! I **scored** a goal in soccer," Max said.

"Well done!" Mom said. She gave Max an apple and then a bowl of soup. "Could you take this soup to Ella, please? She has a bad cold."

Max took his apple and the bowl of soup into the family room. Ella was sitting on the sofa with a blanket pulled up to her chin. There were tissues scattered all around her. Her eyes were red and puffy.

"Here is some soup," Max said. He got up to leave, but then he heard Ella **sniff**. He realized that she was crying. "What's the matter?" he asked.

"I had to come home from school early," Ella said.

"That's not so bad," Max said, taking a bite of his apple.

"It is bad! I missed the zoo trip," Ella said, sniffing again. She looked unhappy.

Max knew that Ella had been really looking forward to going to the zoo. For weeks, she had been talking about all the different animals her class would see.

Max **chewed** on his apple. "Maybe I could be your **entertainment**, instead of the animals at the zoo. I could make you laugh," he said.

"How will you do that?" Ella asked.

STOP AND CHECK

Why was Ella upset?

Chapter 2
Try Again, Max

Max thought about how he could make Ella laugh. Suddenly, he had an idea.

"You couldn't go to the zoo today, but maybe I can bring the zoo to you," Max said. "Zoo animals make funny noises and funny faces. I can act them out for you! It'll make you laugh."

"Okay," Ella said, "I guess that could work."

First, Max decided to act like a lion. He made his hands into claws. "Roar!" he yelled, and then he **lunged** toward Ella.

"That's not funny. That's scary!" Ella said.

"Sorry!" Max said. "I'll try a different animal."

Max made his hands into a beak.

"What's that?" Ella asked.

"What's that?" Max **repeated**, moving his beak as he talked.

"Why are you copying me?" Ella asked.

"Why are you copying me?" Max repeated.

"Are you a parrot?"

"Are you a parrot?"

"That's not funny, Max. That's **annoying**!" Ella said.

"Okay, I'll try again," Max said, sighing.

Max **slithered** across the floor "Sssss!" he said.

"You're a snake," Ella said, "but there's nothing **humorous** or funny about snakes."

Max sat on the sofa and scratched his head. Making Ella laugh was harder than he'd thought it would be.

STOP AND CHECK

Why didn't Ella laugh at Max's animals?

Chapter 3
Monkey Business

"What am I doing wrong?" Max said out loud. He thought for a minute. "I know! I need a funnier animal!" he cried.

"Monkeys are funny," Ella said.

"Great idea!" Max said.

Max got off the sofa and **crouched** on the floor like a monkey. "Ooh-oooh, ah-aah!" he said.

Ella began to smile.

Max leaped up onto the sofa. "Ooh-oooh, ah-aah!" he said scratching his armpits.

Ella started to **giggle**.

Mom came into the family room to see what was going on. Max hopped over to her and pretended to scratch her back. Soon, Mom was giggling, too.

STOP AND CHECK

Why did Max need a funnier animal?

"Come here, silly monkey!" Mom said.

Max shook his head, ran into the kitchen, and came back eating a banana.

Max offered a banana to Ella. "Ooh-oooh, ah-aah?" he asked.

"No, silly monkey! I don't want a banana," Ella said, giggling.

Max **shrugged** his shoulders and ate the rest of his banana. Then he leaped around the room scratching his armpits. He had found out how to make Ella laugh. The more **ridiculous** he acted, the funnier he was. Max jumped onto the sofa and **tickled** Ella until she couldn't stop laughing.

"Monkeys can't tickle!" Ella said.

"I know, but I'm not a monkey anymore. I'm just Max!" Max said, and he laughed, too.

STOP AND CHECK

How did Max make Ella laugh?

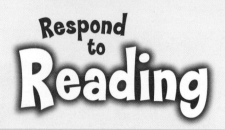

Respond to Reading

Summarize

Summarize the important events in *Funny Faces*. Use details from the text. Your chart may help you.

Details

↓

Point of View

Text Evidence

1. Reread Chapter 2. What does Ella think about Max's efforts to make her laugh? Use details in the story in your answer. POINT OF VIEW

2. Find the word *scattered* on page 3. What does it mean? What clues help you figure it out? VOCABULARY

3. Write about how Max tries to understand how Ella is feeling. Does he do a good job or a bad job? Use details from the text in your answer. WRITE ABOUT READING

Compare Texts
Read a funny poem about a surprise birthday gift.

My Cheeky Puppy

"Happy birthday," said Mom, giving me a box.
Was it a computer or a year's worth of socks?
But computers don't bark and socks don't kick.
The present jumped out and gave me a lick!

What should I name my lovable new pup?
I smiled as he wagged his tail and jumped up.
His eyes were bright and his coat was tip-top.
But look at those ears! I named him Flip Flop.

I opened more gifts—a book, a puzzle, a tie.
And while we were busy Flip passed us all by.
He went to the kitchen and made for the cake.
When time came to cut it, we saw our mistake.

"We'll train him well! He'll learn to be good,"
I promised my mother, hoping that we could.
Mom stared at my puppy, all covered in drool.
"That dog needs to go to obedience school!"

The trainer looked sternly at crazy Flip Flop.
"I'll get him to sit still, to roll, and to drop!"
She whistled and yelled, but he wouldn't obey.
My Flip Flop ran in circles, and then ran away.

Sad and disheartened, with heads hanging low,
We decided to call it a day and just go.
I caught Flip Flop, leashed him, and then
We began walking home to tell Mom, when...

The Gray Street bullies jumped out of a tree!
They were older, tougher, and bigger than me
—nasty, naughty, mean through and through.
I shook and I trembled. Oh, what could I do?

Flip Flop to the rescue—that lovable pup!
He barked, growled, and chased them back up.
They stayed in the tree for the rest of the day.
And Flip Flop and I? We ran off to play!

 Make Connections

What events does the author include in
My Cheeky Puppy to make readers laugh?
What made you laugh? ESSENTIAL QUESTION

Who is funnier, Max or the puppy?
Explain your answer. TEXT TO TEXT

Focus on
Literary Elements

Rhyme Poetry is language that is arranged into patterns. Some poems rhyme. A poem that tells a story is called a narrative poem. Narrative poems often rhyme. A rhyme pattern can give a poem a sense of moving forward.

Read and Find *My Cheeky Puppy* is a narrative poem written in rhyme. The words at the ends of the lines rhyme. For example, in lines 1 and 2, the words *box* and *socks* rhyme; in lines 3 and 4, the words *kick* and *lick* rhyme.

Your Turn

Find the rhyming words on pages 18 and 19. Then read the poem aloud to hear the rhymes clearly.